WHY?

SMALL GROUP STUDY GUIDE

PURSUING ANSWERS TO LIFE'S BIGGEST QUESTIONS

Published by Pursuit, Inc.
1001 New Beginnings Drive
Henderson, NV 89011
www.pursuit.org

ISBN 978-0-9773975-1-8

ISBN 0-9773975-1-3

Cover design and book layout by PlainJoe Studios in Corona, CA.

Printed in Canada

10 9 8 7 6

Introduction

Welcome to the six-week video study of WHY> Pursuing Answers to Life's Biggest Questions. This study guide is designed for your small group to use as you view the video teaching on each week's topic. Each study covers a different big, important question. Following each small group study you should read the next seven days of readings in the WHY> Book. These readings will help you dig a little deeper into each of the big questions.

Throughout the next six weeks your group will be looking at some of the biggest questions ever asked. You'll discuss and read about the questions that have puzzled mankind for thousands of years. The next six weeks have the potential to be a significant part of your spiritual journey. How you come to understand and answer these questions will have a huge effect on your life in the years to come. This introduction will help you get off to a good start. The following is what you'll find in each of the six lessons:

1. **Introduction to the Topic.** Each week begins with an introductory paragraph or two to help you get acquainted with the topic of the day. It would be helpful for you or a group member to read these paragraphs in order to prepare your group for the topic. This is also a great time to pray. Ask God to lead and guide you and your group as you study the lesson.

2. **Opening Up.** This section will give you a few questions related to the topic, and it is a great way to help group members get to know one another and focus their attention on the topic of the day. You can use all of the questions or just one, but remember, none of the group members have to answer a question if they don't want to. Group members feel safer when they're given the freedom to pass on answering a question that makes them uncomfortable.

3. **Looking Back.** After week one, take a moment to review what you studied and read during the previous week. You will be amazed at the insight the Holy Spirit has given to your group members, and how the insight of one will teach another.

4. **Video & Notes.** This study is intended to accompany a video lesson. There are note pages in the study guide which will help you and your group to follow along with the teaching.

5. **Digging In.** This section is designed to help your group dig deeper into God's Word and the topic of the study. Again, don't feel like you need to use every question. Use the questions that are best for you and your group, and feel free to add some questions of your own. Note to group leaders/hosts: It's best for group leaders to view the video and answer these questions prior to the group meeting. This is a great way to prepare to lead the study each week.

6. **Living Out.** This part of the lesson is designed to help each small group member apply the truth of the lesson to his or her life. Again, feel free to pick and choose among the questions.

7. **Lifting Up.** This section introduces a prayer thought for your group. Be sure to spend some time each week praying for one another in your group. Group members can also be paired up to pray for one another during the week, but remember, don't ask anyone to pray if they're uncomfortable with it.

8. **Memory Verse.** Each week, there's a suggested memory verse. Have fun, challenge each other, and encourage your fellow group members to memorize the weekly verse. Be sure to stay positive, and celebrate those who memorized the verse rather than draw attention to those who didn't.

9. **Optional Assignment.** An optional assignment is provided at the end of each lesson. It is designed to be completed during the week to help you focus on the upcoming topic for the next group gathering.

One last note to small group leaders/hosts: Never feel like you have to get through all of the questions in the small group study. It's up to you to manage your overall group time. Feel free to pick just one or two questions in each area, and use only those that work well within your time frame. We want this group time to be a rich and rewarding experience for everyone involved. If you run into any roadblocks or problems that are getting in the way of this being a great experience, ask for help. Talk to your small group pastor sooner rather than later, and seek assistance in caring for the problem.

We hope you all enjoy the study. Have fun pursuing the answers to life's biggest questions.

About the Authors and Editors

Jud Wilhite, Author and Contributing Editor

Jud is the Senior Pastor of Central Christian Church in Las Vegas, NV. Through his leadership, Central has become a pioneering community of faith that has reached in excess of thirteen thousand in attendance. He has authored several books including his latest, Stripped: Uncensored Grace on the Streets of Vegas. His message and inspiration to exhibit extreme grace is found in WHY> and other Pursuit books and resources.

Mike Bodine, Contributing Editor

Mike is the Senior Leader of Central Christian Church in Las Vegas, NV. Through his leadership, Central has become a church that reaches and disciples people through radical alignment, a process he and Pursuit call ChurchSync™. ChurchSync™ principles are wired into Pursuit Campaigns and other Pursuit resources and are one of the reasons these materials are so effective at reaching and discipling people.

Bart Rendel, Executive Editor

Bart is the President of Pursuit Ministries. Pursuit grew out of the ministry of Central Christian Church in Las Vegas, NV and exists to help other churches respond to the Great Commission by teaching and resourcing them in the principles of uncensored grace and radical alignment. Bart is also the Executive Editor of the WHY> campaign, book, and equipping materials.

The Pursuit Team, Authors

A great portion of this book was written by a talented team of authors whose passion is to see people equipped to defend their faith or get answers to their most burning spiritual questions. The Pursuit Team has written several other books and studies dedicated to reaching people and teaching them about the life-changing and practical truths of Scripture. Look for more life-transformational studies and resources at www.pursuit.org.

Table of Contents

GATHERING 1

WHY AM I HERE?

Is there a God? Can I really trust the Bible? Why is there pain in the world if God is a loving God? How can Jesus be the only way to heaven? Doesn't science contradict the Bible? At some point in life these questions float through everyone's mind. There's a very real longing inside of you to know if God is really out there and if He has the answers to life's questions.

"He [God] has also set eternity in the hearts of men; yet they cannot fathom what God has done from beginning to end" (Ecclesiastes 3:11, NIV). You have a place in your heart that is made for eternity. This is why you raise spiritual questions. You're made to be aware of God's presence and to know Him in a personal way, but you'll never be able to fully understand Him while you're here on earth. You won't comprehend every eternal question, but you can find the answers you need to move on to the next step in your spiritual journey.

Welcome to the next forty days of pursuing God. The intent of this series is to tackle some important spiritual questions about God and to cultivate new friendships along the way. It's time to take the first step. Are you ready?

OPENING UP (Select one or two of these for your group to discuss.)

> Introduce yourself and share where you are originally from.

> What is your favorite food?

VIDEO NOTES (Jot down some insights from the teaching.)

Why Am I Here?

"I didn't understand how all the pieces fit together."

1. The five most common questions:

> Why Should I Believe in God in the First Place?

> Why Should I Trust the Bible?

> Why Is the World So Messed Up?

> Why Is There Conflict between Science and the Bible?

> Why Jesus?

2. Five opportunities for the next forty days:

> P___________________ each week.

> Commit to your g____________________.

> Read a c____________________each day.

> M________________________ a Bible verse.

> P_______________________ for a friend.

"The more you put into the group, the more you'll get out of it."

DIGGING IN (Discuss one or two of these questions.)

> As discussed in the video, can you relate to the teacher's experience with church? What were your thoughts about the importance of being involved with God when you were younger?

> If you could meet God face-to-face and ask Him one question, what would it be?

> Why does God want us to ask hard questions? Why do you think God doesn't give an answer to every question we ask?

> How comfortable or confident are you with answering a difficult spiritual question that a friend or co-worker might ask? (e.g. Why did God allow the tsunami to take so many lives?)

LIVING OUT (Discuss one or two of these questions to discover the impact of God's truth on your life.)

> Describe your spiritual journey. How have you searched for answers to your spiritual questions?

> Take some time to talk about the upcoming weeks in this study. When and where will your group meet? Who is going to bring the refreshments next week?

> Review the forty day commitment:
Attend weekend services or listen to the CDs if you're unable to attend.
Participate in a WHY> small group.
Read the WHY> Book.
Memorize one scripture each week.
Pray for one or more seeking friends every week and look for an opportunity to give them a WHY> Magazine or an invitation to church.

LIFTING UP (Share a time of prayer and praise with your group.)

God, I have so many questions in my heart for You.
Please take the next forty days of my life and fill me with answers.
I want to know You better than ever.
I give this month to You.
AMEN.

MEMORY VERSE

"For the Son of Man came to seek and to save what was lost."
- Luke 19:10 (NIV)

OPTIONAL ASSIGNMENT (Get ready for next time.)

Next week we'll talk about the existence of God. Spend ten minutes outdoors before the next session. Look at the beauty of nature around you, and record some of the things you see supporting the notion that there is a God. Bring the list to your group meeting next week.

NOTES

NOTES

GATHERING 2>

WHY SHOULD I BELIEVE IN GOD IN THE FIRST PLACE?

I know a guy who moved to Las Vegas in the summer and was so impressed with the desert that he decided to take a long walk in the sun; however, he didn't take any water with him. Would you call that foolish? How about the well-meaning grandfather at the M&M factory on the Las Vegas strip who said to his grandkids, "Go ahead and fill up a bag of M&Ms to take home!" He spent forty-three dollars on three small bags of candy. Would you call that foolish?

There are a lot of foolish things you and I can do. Some are just embarrassing, others lead us into sin, but the most foolish thing anyone can do is outlined in this Bible verse: "The fool says in his heart, 'There is no God'" (Psalm 53:1, NIV).

Is there really a God who's the supreme ruler of the universe, who's bigger than everything, and who loves and cares about you? Is He really out there?

There's only one way to find out for certain: to die! Inevitably, you'll know the truth of the matter, but hopefully that day is a long way off. So until then, we can look at a few things that build a convincing argument for the existence of a very real and loving Almighty God.

Nature demonstrates a design and balance that is indicative of a Creator. Changed lives of those who follow Christ show a positive transformation that can only be explained by a personal and powerful Savior. The Bible acknowledges and assumes that God exists. Jesus came to earth to show us the Father. So many things point to the existence of God that it would take more faith to deny Him than to believe in Him!

How about you? How do you answer these persistent questions we all ask? Enjoy the company of your new friends as you share your thoughts and observations on why you should believe in God in the first place.

OPENING UP (Select one or two questions for your group to discuss.)

> When did you first wonder about whether or not God exists? Did you always believe or are you still wondering?

> What shaped your perception of God as you were growing up? How did you get the picture of God that you now carry in your heart and mind?

LOOKING BACK (Reflect on last week's lesson.)

> Did you do last week's assignment? Where did you go to do it? What did you observe about God from viewing nature?

> Last week we asked, "Why am I here?" Have you pondered that further? What are your thoughts?

VIDEO NOTES (Jot down some insights from the teaching.)

Why Should I Believe in God in the First Place?

"It's hard to escape the sense that there is a God. Every civilization around the world tends to believe in either a god or gods."

1. Reasons from the H____________________.

> The u________________ has so much d__________________.

> "I'm convinced that it takes more faith to believe our world was created by chance than it does to believe it was created by a Creator."

2. Reasons from the H_____________________.

> "So I fell to my knees and surrendered to God."

> "My greatest argument for the existence of God is simply myself."

DIGGING IN (Open your Bible and discuss one or two of these questions.)

> Read Genesis 1:1. Does the Bible begin with an assumption that God exists or an argument for His existence? Why?

> Do you agree or disagree with this statement? "There's enough evidence in the order and design of this world to believe in a Creator." Check out these verses to support your thoughts.

> Psalm 19:1

> Romans 1:20

> What are some of the other ways that God reveals Himself to us?

> Hebrews 1:1-2

> Psalm 66:16-20

> 2 Timothy 3:16-17

> Read Exodus 3:13-14. How was Moses instructed to identify the One who sent him to deliver the Israelites? What is implied in this name? What do these verses teach us about who God is?

> Psalm 90:2

> Revelation 22:13

LIVING OUT (Discuss one or two of these questions to discover the impact of God's truth on your life.)

> What would life be like for you if God did not exist? Think of a time when He was close to you, and then try to imagine what would have happened without Him.

> What part of the teacher's personal story can you relate to most? What has your spiritual journey been like so far?

> If you know God exists, what is He like? Share some of His character traits that mean the most to you.

LIFTING UP (Share a time of prayer and praise with your group.)

Dear Lord, thank You that You exist
and that You desire to have a relationship with me.
The wonders of Your world speak of Your power and beauty.
The ache in my soul demands that You are there pursuing me.
I marvel at Your love and Your grace.
Help me to live this week with a clear awareness of Your presence.
I praise You for Jesus' sake.
AMEN.

MEMORY VERSE

"Now all has been heard; here is the conclusion of the matter: Fear God and keep his commandments." - Ecclesiastes 12:13 (NIV)

OPTIONAL ASSIGNMENT (Get ready for next time.)

This week's readings address a lot of questions about the Bible. Here are just a few of those questions: Is the Bible reliable? Are the right books in the Bible? How do we know it's the same as it was two thousand years ago? What evidence is there that the Bible is true? As you meditate on the daily readings, write any questions you can think of. Bring those questions to the small group and discuss them next week.

NOTES

GATHERING 3

WHY SHOULD I TRUST THE BIBLE?

Assembling a bicycle without an instruction manual can be more than a little annoying. This exasperating experience can turn from enthusiasm to frustration to depression in a matter of hours. This is true for any project that is attempted without the proper owner's manual. The new computer owner, the driveway mechanic, or the do it yourself homeowner can go only so far before they need to consult the manufacturer's instructions. How does part #235 attach to part #236 anyway?

If you visit your local maternity ward and sneak a peek at the newborn babies, you'll notice their pink faces and cute little toes, but there's one thing you won't find—that's right—there are no owner's manuals in the bassinets. So, are we to assume there's no book of instructions for living this life?

Long before you were born and placed into the nursery, God inscribed the necessary truths you would need for living. It's called the Bible, which literally means books. It contains history, poetry, letters, and prophecy. Most importantly, it provides clear direction for your life. The Bible is the Word of God revealed to humanity. It is God's instruction manual for living.

But can you really trust it? Has it been corrupted through the years? Is there evidence that supports its claim to be the authoritative Word of God? Or is it simply a collection of myths and legends that have no bearing on the twenty-first century?

Good questions! Let's see what we can find out this week in our study.

OPENING UP (Select one or two questions for your group to discuss.)

> Share something unique about yourself that the group may not know.

> Have you ever tried to assemble something without the instructions? How far did you get? What is one of the hardest things you've ever had to assemble?

LOOKING BACK (Reflect on last week's lesson.)

> Are you convinced of the existence of God? Where have you seen intelligent design this week?

> Did you do last week's assignment? How many Bibles do you own? How many translations? Do you have a favorite verse?

> Did you memorize the last few weeks' memory verses? Have someone recite them and give plenty of applause and encouragement.

VIDEO NOTES (Jot down some insights from the teaching.)

Why Should I Trust the Bible?

"The Bible is a historical work, it didn't just miraculously appear."

1. Is the Bible full of myths and legends?

> The Bible's sixty-six books were written over a ___________ year span, by around ___________ different authors, on ___________ different continents, and in ___________ different languages.

> It has been published in over __________ languages and dialects.

> Americans spend an average of ___________ a year on the Bible.

2. Do Bible teachings work?

> “Therefore everyone who hears these words of mine and puts them into _______________ is like a _______________ man who built his house on the rock” (Matthew 7:24, NIV).

> “When people I care about have to make a critical decision in life, I direct them to the Bible.”

DIGGING IN (Open your Bible and discuss one or two of these questions.)

> According to 2 Timothy 3:16-17, how was the scripture produced and what are the results of following its teachings?

> What was Jesus’ view of scripture? How does His use of the Old Testament verify the authority and reliability of the Bible?

> Matthew 5:18

> Matthew 4:4

> Luke 24:44

> Read 2 Peter 3:15-16. What was the Apostle Peter's view of Paul's writing? How does this add confirmation to the reliability of the New Testament?

> Consider this quote from Jewish archeologist Nelson Glueck: "It may be stated categorically that no archeological discovery has ever controverted a biblical reference." What is he saying? Do you know of any further evidence that supports this statement?

LIVING OUT (Discuss one or two of these questions to discover the impact of God's truth on your life.)

> What is your view of scripture? How reliable do you think it is? Is there anything you're still skeptical about relating to the Bible? Talk with your group about it. They may have helpful ideas for you.

> Many people are convinced of the Bible's truth because it has changed their lives in some way. If it has changed your life in some way, share how it happened with your group. What effect has this had on your life since then?

> Discuss the two men in Matthew 7:24-27 that were mentioned in the video teaching. Did only one have the Word of God or did they both have it? What is the major difference between the two men in the story?

LIFTING UP (Share a time of prayer and praise with your group.)

Almighty God, grant us grace to hear Jesus Christ, the heavenly bread,
preached throughout the world and help us truly understand Him.
May all evil, heretical, and human doctrines be cut off,
while your Word as the living bread is distributed.
AMEN.

-Martin Luther

MEMORY VERSE

"Therefore everyone who hears these words of mine and puts them into practice is like a wise man who built his house on the rock." - Matthew 7:24 (NIV)

OPTIONAL ASSIGNMENT (Get ready for next time.)

Next week, we'll discuss the issue of evil in the world. Why does a loving God allow the world to be so painful? Look in your local newspaper to find examples of evil (you won't have to look very hard). See if there are any articles or editorials that raise the question of where God is in the midst of disaster and conflict. Bring your results to the next group gathering.

NOTES

GATHERING 4›

WHY IS THE WORLD SO MESSED UP?

It's hard to erase the images from our minds. The mass graves. The distraught parents searching for their children. The debris. The gaping holes where villages once stood.

Since that December day when a massive tsunami ravaged Southeastern Asia, much of the world has reeled in stunned horror as they have watched the wreckage unfold on their television screens. Whether in the heart of the devastation or sitting comfortably in a living room, the global community inevitably raised the age-old questions—Where was God? And how could He let this happen?

The same questions were raised after 9/11 when Americans watched the twin towers of the World Trade Center crumble to pieces with thousands of people trapped inside. The answers were clearer then—at least there was someone to blame. But with a natural disaster like the tsunami that indiscriminately killed more than two hundred thousand people, it's tempting to shake your fist at the big guy who's supposed to be in charge.

"If God were good," Christian apologetic C.S. Lewis wrote, "He would wish to make His creatures happy, and if God were almighty, He would be able to do what He wished. But the creatures are not happy. Therefore God lacks either goodness, or power, or both." Therefore, the dilemma becomes: "How can God be loving and sovereign while the world is hurting?"

In the bittersweet journey of life, the hows and whys of our struggles are often shrouded in mystery. The Bible, however, provides a bigger picture. In God's story, we find disobedience of mankind followed by the compassionate rescue of God. The cross of Jesus is the ultimate expression of God sharing in our pain and overcoming it. Today, His presence will strengthen you for any sorrow, and tomorrow He'll wipe away every tear from your eyes.

OPENING UP (Select one or two questions for your group to discuss.)

> What is one of the hardest times you've gone through? What helped you through it?

> Has pain in your life ever turned out for good?

LOOKING BACK (Reflect on last week's lesson.)

> Do you have further questions about the Bible? Ask the group for clarity on one or two of your questions.

> Last week's assignment was to discover examples of evil or trouble in the news. What did you find? What are people saying about God's place in the midst of disaster and conflict?

VIDEO NOTES (Jot down some insights from the teaching.)

Why Is the World So Messed Up?

"Where is God when it hurts? Why doesn't He intervene? Why do horrible things often happen to people who are not horrible?"

1. God's s________________________ helps me make sense of our messed-up world.

> "Sin entered the world. God cursed the ground and they had to leave Eden. The first paradise was closed."

> "Much of the human heartache and pain in our world is not God's fault. It is the fault of people."

> "Heaven will be free from the curse, free from Satan, free from death."

2. God's p__________________ helps me endure this messed-up world.

> "No matter how crazy things get, God works for good."

> "Only the Gospel portrait of God makes sense of the contradictory fact that the world is at once so beautiful and so ugly." -Greg Boyd

DIGGING IN (Open your Bible and discuss one or two of these questions.)

> Read Genesis 3:16-24. What were the consequences of Adam and Eve's disobedience? How does this explain the nature of living in a fallen world where paradise is closed?

> Read Revelation 21:1-4. What will "paradise restored" be like? How does seeing this bigger picture help bring perspective to the troubles of this world?

> Jesus experienced pain and suffering. He understands the human condition. Describe what these verses tell us about Jesus' exposure to difficulty and why He is compassionate toward mankind.

> John 11:35

> Hebrews 4:15

> Mark 15:15-37

> What is the attitude of faith for followers of Christ when evil touches their lives?

> Romans 8:18

> Romans 8:28

> James 1:2-4

LIVING OUT (Discuss one or two of these questions to discover the impact of God's truth on your life.)

> When do you remember God being especially close to you during a time of tragedy or sorrow? How did His presence make a difference in your ability to cope?

> What storms of life are you experiencing now? How can you claim the promise of Romans 8:28 for your situation?

> When is it easier to see God's hand—during the crisis and difficulty or after the darkness has passed? What has been true for you? How does looking back give you perspective?

LIFTING UP (Share a time of prayer and praise with your group.)

We thank You, God, for the story You have given us and the hope it brings.
We thank You for sending Your Son to this earth
and humbling Yourself in order to understand our pain.
We thank You for restoring us to You and giving us the promise
that one day You will wipe every tear from our eyes.
AMEN.

MEMORY VERSE

"And we know that in all things God works for the good of those who love him, who have been called according to his purpose." - Romans 8:28 (NIV)

OPTIONAL ASSIGNMENT (Get ready for next time.)

Next week, we'll explore the conflicts between science and the Bible. Look for references to evolution as you read magazines and watch TV this week. How prevalent is the theory of evolution? Bring your observations to the next group gathering.

NOTES

GATHERING 5›

WHY THE CONFLICT… SCIENCE AND THE BIBLE?

When you see a piece of art, you're right to conclude that there was a painter who created it. You base your decision on the evidence you see—a canvas with colors that combine to make a picture. Because of the facts, you believe there was a painter.

Science is the knowledge of the universe gathered through a process of observation, investigation, and experimentation. Some scientists observe the human body, while others accumulate data from the stars. Oncologists study cancer cells, and oologists study eggs and bird nests. Whatever the field, the information is collected and catalogued to amass a larger base of knowledge to be stored or applied in a practical way.

There are no factual scientific observations that conflict with the Bible. Whenever the Bible gives descriptions in the arenas of anatomy, biology, or astronomy they're consistent with scientific truth. For instance, Isaiah 40:21-22 (NIV) correctly states that the world is a sphere. "Have you not understood since the earth was founded? He sits enthroned above the circle of the earth." This was written long before the discovery that the earth was not flat.

Conflict develops between the Bible and science in two ways:

> **1.** The scientific community proposes theories that are regarded as scientific fact. This is precisely the issue with evolution. The concept that plants, animals, and humans evolved over a long period of time is a theory that cannot be proven. Therefore, what the Bible teaches and what the theory claims are in conflict.
>
> **2.** The Bible records supernatural phenomena that are outside the realm of natural science. Miracles cannot be explained apart from the intervention of a superior being.

Once the facts are in, you will still need to exercise faith. Once you have taken a good look at the painting, you still have to determine whether or not you believe there was a painter. God calls you to look at the data and believe in Him. Science should bolster your faith by providing information and reasoning that points you back to God.

OPENING UP (Select one or two questions for your group to discuss.)

> **>** What were you taught in school: evolution or creation? What made the most sense to you as you were growing up?

> Did you do last week's assignment? What did you observe about the prevailing evolutionary perspective? Where did you see examples of its teachings?

LOOKING BACK (Reflect on last week's lesson.)

> Recite last week's memory verse as a group, then have someone give a personal example of how it was true this week.

> How has your perspective on pain and suffering changed after last week's study? How did you handle it in your life this week?

> Last week's assignment asked you to look for references to evolution in the media. What did you find? How prevalent is the theory today?

VIDEO NOTES (Jot down some insights from the teaching.)

Why the Conflict...Science and the Bible?

"Though God can't be put in a test tube to be probed and experimented, current scientific research has opened new windows for faith."

1. The ________________________ had a beginning.

> "This is an area of faith, but clearly the evidence points to the fact that the universe had a beginning."

> "Isn't it interesting that a document thousands of years old defines the parameters of that which modern science can operate in?"

2. Evolutionary theory does not present an ______________________ case for the origin of life.

> "Whatever your take on evolution, it is a theory, one which is being questioned intensely from many voices in the scientific community, irrespective of their religious beliefs."

> "When it comes to the origin of life, we are dealing in matters of faith, whether you are a scientist or a believer."

DIGGING IN (Open your Bible and discuss one or two of these questions.)

> Is the Bible primarily a scientific document? What is its real purpose? Why is it important that the Bible and scientific facts be compatible?

> Read Genesis 1:1. What is the claim of the Bible concerning God's existence and the beginning of the universe?

> Read Luke 16:19-31. What is Jesus teaching about the nature of faith? Do empirical evidence and facts always produce God-honoring faith?

LIVING OUT (Discuss one or two of these questions to discover the impact of God's truth on your life.)

> What are the dangers in placing your faith in science alone? Where does science fall short in explaining life?

> What other areas of science or the Bible are usually questioned? How do you answer these issues?

> Explain why you agree or disagree with the teacher's statement: "Often what we presuppose when we consider a subject causes us to see the facts differently."

LIFTING UP (Share a time of prayer and praise with your group.)

Dear Lord of the universe. I marvel at Your knowledge of all things.
I worship You for Your majesty reflected in creation.
I exalt Your name for Your grace demonstrated to me.
May I, like the skies, proclaim Your glory.
AMEN.

MEMORY VERSE

"The heavens declare the glory of God; the skies proclaim the work of his hands. Day after day they pour forth speech; night after night they display knowledge."
- Psalm 19:1-2 (NIV)

OPTIONAL ASSIGNMENT (Get ready for next time.)

Next week we'll discuss why Jesus is the only way to God. Look in the phonebook and count how many different religions you can find in the church pages. Bring that number to group if it's more than one.

NOTES

NOTES

GATHERING 6

WHY JESUS?

My wife claims that there's only one way to fill the dishwasher—her way—but that's not true. I load the machine quite differently. I put the bowls on the top and she puts them on the bottom. My brother-in-law thinks there's only one way to get to Wal-Mart—his way—but he's wrong. I've found several other ways to get there. Very few decisions in life are that limited.

Jesus claimed that there was only one way to know the Father—His way. "Jesus answered, 'I am the way and the truth and the life. No one comes to the Father except through me'" (John 14:6, NIV). In this case, Jesus was absolutely right in His exclusive claim. "For there is one God and one mediator between God and men, the man Christ Jesus, who gave himself as a ransom for all men" (1 Timothy 2:5-6, NIV).

On the surface it would appear all religions are basically the same. They're systems of beliefs that promote benevolent behavior and reverent thoughts. They may have a few distinctions, but underneath they appear to be made of the same stuff. A closer investigation, however, will show that all other religions require man to earn his favor with God, but Christianity is based on God giving salvation freely through Christ. Also, Jesus is a unique figure in history. All other religious leaders have died, but Jesus is the only One that died and rose again, setting Him apart as the God He asserted Himself to be.

Sometimes there is only one legitimate option. If you drive from Las Vegas to Barstow, there's only one highway. There are no alternate routes to get there from here. If you want to go to Barstow and stay on pavement, then you have one exclusive option—Highway 15. That's very much the picture of Jesus. He is the one and only way to eternal life. There are no other viable options. No other roads will get you there. No other religions will do the job. That's because Christianity is a relationship and not a religion. Do you have a relationship with Jesus? Are you on your way down the only path that leads to God?

OPENING UP (Select one or two questions for your group to discuss.)

> **>** You have spent several weeks with your small group in this study. What have you learned about each other? Go around the group and tell each person what you appreciate about them.

> How many religions did you study before you discovered Christianity? How many of them claimed to be exclusive?

LOOKING BACK (Reflect on last week's lesson.)

> How did last week's lesson help you understand the relationship between science and the Bible?

> What did you find in the phonebook as a result of last week's assignment? How many religions are available in your community? Why does having so many options make the pursuit of a relationship with God so confusing?

VIDEO NOTES (Jot down some insights from the teaching.)

Why Jesus?

The uniqueness of Christianity is rooted in the uniqueness of Jesus Himself.

1. Jesus claimed to be ______________________________. (John 5:17-18)

2. Jesus claimed to have ______________________________. (John 5:21)

3. Jesus claimed to be ______________________________. (John 5:22)

4. Jesus claimed ______________________________. (John 5:23)

5. Jesus claimed the ___________________________. (John 5:24)

6. Jesus claimed to be ________________________. (John 5:26-27)

"If Jesus is who He claims to be, as my Creator He rightfully deserves my allegiance, obedience, and worship." -Lee Strobel

DIGGING IN (Open your Bible and discuss one or two of these questions.)

> In Matthew 16:15 (NIV), Jesus asks His disciples, "Who do men say that I am?" How would you answer that question today?

> The video listed several of the claims of Christ found in John 5:17-27. What else does the Bible teach about Him?

> John 1:1, 1:14

> Isaiah 9:6

> Hebrews 1:3

> Matthew 20:28

> Colossians 2:9

> Revelation 1:18

> Read Acts 4:12. What does this verse teach about the exclusivity of Christ? If other world religions are also true, what does that do to this statement of scripture?

> Describe each of these opinions of Jesus:

> He is a legend.

> He is a liar.

> He is a lunatic.

> He is Lord.

LIVING OUT (Discuss one or two of these questions to discover the impact of God's truth on your life.)

> Have you struggled with accepting the exclusiveness of Jesus? Where are you now in your understanding of His claims?

> Why is it impossible to believe Jesus was simply a good man? How would that be an inconsistent conclusion from looking at His life and teachings?

> What examples of Jesus' healthy mental state can you find? How does this demonstrate He wasn't crazy?

LIFTING UP (Share a time of prayer and praise with your group.)

O Lamb of God. Thank You for Your compassion
and Your sacrifice in my place.
I call on You as my Savior. I worship You as my King.
I bow before You as Lord of my life.
AMEN.

MEMORY VERSE

"Jesus answered, 'I am the way and the truth and the life. No one comes to the Father except through me.'" - John 14:6 (NIV)

OPTIONAL ASSIGNMENT (Get ready for what's next.)

Now that you've finished this journey, find out what your church is offering for groups and classes that will start you on the next step to being a devoted follower of Jesus Christ. Keep growing. Stay on the path. Determine your next step and take it!

NOTES

NOTES

NOTES

WHY>

FORMS AND HELPFUL PAGES

SMALL GROUP PLANNING GUIDE

This guide is to assist small group leaders in planning and communicating with regard to the details of a group.

Leader: ______________________________

Names of people in the small group:

1. ______________________________

2. ______________________________

3. ______________________________

4. ______________________________

5. ______________________________

6. ______________________________

7. ______________________________

8. ______________________________

9. ______________________________

10. ______________________________

Group Expectations: (Check all that apply.)

- ☐ We expect it will be a priority for all members to attend regularly scheduled group meetings, to call if they cannot attend, and we expect that every effort will be made to arrive on time.

- ☐ We expect that the members of our group will spend time together to build relationships outside of regularly scheduled group meetings.

- ☐ We expect that all group members will be open, honest, and willing to participate in group discussions.
- ☐ We expect that group members will keep all discussions confidential.
- ☐ We expect all members to be available to one another in a time of need. Group members have permission to call one another for spiritual, physical, or emotional help and support, even at inconvenient times.
- ☐ We expect group members to hold one another accountable for spiritual growth and goals that individuals have set for themselves and have shared with the group.
- ☐ Other expectations: ______________________________

  ____

Details of Group and Group Meetings: (Check all that apply and fill in the blanks.)

- ☐ We will be an open group until (date) ______________
- ☐ We will limit the number of people in our group to ______________
- ☐ Day we will meet: ______________________________
- ☐ How often we will meet: ______________________________
- ☐ Where we will meet: ______________________________
- ☐ Our meetings begin at (time) __________ and end at __________
- ☐ We plan to handle childcare in our group by: ______________
- ☐ How we plan to handle worship/prayer as a group: ______________

  ____

☐ How we plan to handle refreshments as a group: ____________________

____

____

Mission and Outreach:

How will our group reach out to others who are not a part of our group? (i.e. service, evangelism, specific projects): ____________________

____

____

Leadership Responsibilities:

List those who will be responsible for the following jobs that apply to your group:

Leader/Facilitator ____________________

Apprentice or Co-leader ____________________

Prayer Coordinator ____________________

Refreshment Coordinator ____________________

Mission Project Coordinator ____________________

Secretary (fills out monthly Small Group Report) ____________________

Activity Coordinator ____________________

Other leadership responsibilities: ____________________

☐ Our group does not have an apprentice/co-leader, but we agree to pray and look for an apprentice from within our group.

SMALL GROUP MEMBER INFORMATION

Name(s): ____

Address: ____

____

Phone: Home ______________________

Cell ______________________

Other ______________________

E-mail: ____

Birthday(s): ________________ Anniversary: ________________

- -

Name(s): ____

Address: ____

____

Phone: Home ______________________

Cell ______________________

Other ______________________

E-mail: ____

Birthday(s): ________________ Anniversary: ________________

Name(s): ____

Address: ____

____

Phone: Home ______________________

Cell ______________________

Other ______________________

E-mail: ____

Birthday(s): __________________ Anniversary: __________________

- -

Name(s): ____

Address: ____

____

Phone: Home ______________________

Cell ______________________

Other ______________________

E-mail: ____

Birthday(s): __________________ Anniversary: __________________

Name(s): ____

Address: ____

____

Phone: Home ______________________

Cell ______________________

Other ______________________

E-mail: ____

Birthday(s): __________________ Anniversary: __________________

- -

Name(s): ____

Address: ____

____

Phone: Home ______________________

Cell ______________________

Other ______________________

E-mail: ____

Birthday(s): __________________ Anniversary: __________________

Name(s): ____

Address: ____

____

Phone: Home ______________________

Cell ______________________

Other ______________________

E-mail: ____

Birthday(s): __________________ Anniversary: __________________

- -

Name(s): ____

Address: ____

____

Phone: Home ______________________

Cell ______________________

Other ______________________

E-mail: ____

Birthday(s): __________________ Anniversary: __________________

Name(s): ____

Address: ____

____

Phone: Home ______________________

Cell ______________________

Other ______________________

E-mail: ____

Birthday(s): __________________ Anniversary: __________________

- -

Name(s): ____

Address: ____

____

Phone: Home ______________________

Cell ______________________

Other ______________________

E-mail: ____

Birthday(s): __________________ Anniversary: __________________

Name(s): ____

Address: ____

____

Phone: Home ______________________

Cell ______________________

Other ______________________

E-mail: ____

Birthday(s): ________________ Anniversary: ________________

- -

Name(s): ____

Address: ____

____

Phone: Home ______________________

Cell ______________________

Other ______________________

E-mail: ____

Birthday(s): ________________ Anniversary: ________________

MEMORY VERSES

GATHERING 1
"For the Son of Man came to seek and to save what was lost" (Luke 19:10, NIV).

GATHERING 2
"Now all has been heard; here is the conclusion of the matter: Fear God and keep his commandments" (Ecclesiastes 12:13, NIV).

GATHERING 3
"Therefore everyone who hears these words of mine and puts them into practice is like a wise man who built his house on the rock" (Matthew 7:24, NIV).

GATHERING 4
"And we know that in all things God works for the good of those who love him, who have been called according to his purpose" (Romans 8:28, NIV).

GATHERING 5
"The heavens declare the glory of God; the skies proclaim the work of his hands. Day after day they pour forth speech; night after night they display knowledge" (Psalm 19:1-2, NIV).

GATHERING 6
"Jesus answered, 'I am the way and the truth and the life. No one comes to the Father except through me'" (John 14:6, NIV).